Options Trading Crash Course

The Complete Crash Course To Learn How Investing And Making Money Online with Trading Options in 7 Days or Less!

By

Joseph Stone

Contents

Introduction

It's all about customization when it comes to investing with options. The stakes can be high, but so can be the risk, and you have many options. However, getting started is difficult, and costly mistakes can be made. Options trading is primarily aimed at the do-it-yourself investor. Option traders stand typically self-guided investors, which means they do not work with some financial advisor for managing the options trading profiles. You have complete control over your trading decisions and transactions as a do-it-yourself (D.I.Y.) investor. However, this does not imply that you are alone. There are numerous online communities where traders can discuss the current market outlook and option trading strategies. Most newcomers begin with stock options. Stock options, also known as equities options, are a type of option that is based on equities. Stock options are listed in the form of a quote on exchanges like the NYSE. Before you decide, it's critical to understand the specifics of stock options quotes, such as the cost and expiration date. A stock options quote is a compact form of detailed information. You can quickly understand important details of the option contract, such as the type, cost, and expiration date, once you understand what each segment represents. Contracts that give the owner the right to buy or sell an asset at a set price for a set period are known as options. Depending on the type of options contract, that period could be as short as a day or if a couple of years. Fortunately, standard option contracts are limited to only two types: call and put. Options can be used in various ways, including to speculate or mitigate risk, and they can be traded on a variety of underlying securities. Equities, indexes, and exchange-traded funds (ETFs) are the most common underlying securities (Exchange Traded Funds). There are several distinctions between index-based options and those depending on equities & ETFs. Before you begin trading, it's critical to understand the differences. As you will read this book, you will educate yourself on various aspects of options and options trading.

CHAPTER 1: Types of Investments

The premise behind all investment decisions is to generate money smartly and efficiently while keeping the risk factors to the minimum. As a prudent investor, you must select the best investment opportunity from the available options. You, being the investor, will be guided in your quest by researching for answers to different critical questions such as:

- What investment option offers the most secure return concerning Investment Time?
- Where is that particular investment option currently in its Business Cycle?
- When is the best time for committing the Investment Amount?

Prices do not move in a straight line, and the price activity is shaped by scores of factors stemming from changes in political and industrial policies to frequent shifts in international business supply and demand factors. This standard operating procedure is usually also followed in the Forex, Stock and Option Markets, with another crucial factor that attempts to seek and investigate the reasons behind such an investment decision. Succinctly, an investment decision revolves around the three W's.

1.1 What to Buy or Trade

Once you have arrived at an investment or trading decision, the next rational step is to set off a comparative analysis of different available investment options based on their liquidity. Liquidity is an attribute of an investment or trading option that makes it easily accessible during the buying and selling process. This first step will assist you in unraveling the best-performing investment or trading option based on its past and current performance.

1.2 Why Buy or Trade

The ensuing step should be to perform a threadbare analysis of investment options based on earning potential, market competitiveness versus exclusivity, price behavior etc.

1.3 When to Buy or Trade

Finally, a decision must be made on the investment time. Prices move in a wave-like pattern. This wave-like pattern owes its formation to the crest and troughs that appear on a graph due to respective highs and lows attained during a particular period. These highs and lows are materialized because of the respective bullish and bearish spells in the stocks and commodities. This is because all business cycles follow a cyclical movement of Growth (Expansion), Peak (Top), Decline (Contraction), Recession (Trough) and then back to Expansion. Commit your investment to an astronomically performing stock or commodity at the peak of the business cycle. You should be ready to be flushed out from the market bare-handed as peaks do not remain intact for a long time and stun the investors by the sharp downturn. Thus, the timing of investment is the most critical factor which must be worked out astutely. An investment or trading decision, no matter how smart, could result in the wiping of funds if not exquisitely timed.

1.4. Long-term vs. Short-term Investments

When devising an investment strategy, you must consider both long- and short-term objectives and select investments that reflect your goals. Finding the right balance is crucial to building a portfolio that works for you.

1.4.1 When should you choose long-term over short-term investments?

Long-term investments are those that you expect to keep for a long period. Long-term investments are assets such as stocks and real estate that you intend to hold for a long time. They allow you to grow your portfolio because you know you won't need the money for a long time.

1.4.2 Your retirement is more than 20 years away

If you're more than two decades away from retirement, there's still a long way to go before you stop working. Long-term investments, such as stocks, are a good asset class to build wealth over decades because they require time to grow.

1.4.3 You need a plan for seven to 10 years in the future

Another thing to think about is your timeline. Low- and medium-risk portfolios are common in financial plans for the next seven years. However, when you get in the 7-10 years range, you will believe in riskier assets. In general, long-term investments such as stocks can be used for the money you won't need for a longer period. When you need money, dividend stocks are a good option for medium-term goals because they pay out regularly and can grow.

1.4.4 You want protection from inflation

Long-term investments may also be preferable if you want to beat inflation or be protected from it. Long-term investments, such as stocks, are often regarded as less safe than other assets, but they offer a higher potential rate of return over time, giving you a better chance of preserving your purchasing power.

1.4.5 When should you choose short-term over long-term investments?

Short-term investments are those that you intend to use to achieve financial objectives in a short period. Rather than building your portfolio, you may require the funds to provide a steady source of income. Bonds, cash, and annuities are examples of short-term investments. There are some circumstances in which short-term investments make sense.

1.4.6 When you need money soon

Short-term investments may make sense when saving for shorter-term goals, such as a down payment on a home. Specific deposit accounts, e.g., can offer a fixed rate of return while also allowing you to pull out funds whenever you want. You can put your cash into the money market short-term bonds or mutual funds and expect to be able to access it for a short-term goal without fear of a loss in the market.

1.4.7 You are looking for perpetual income

Short-term investments are frequently linked to a steady income. When you know, you'll need consistent income, investing in high-rated bonds and other assets can help. While the return isn't as high as it could be with some stocks, you have a better chance of dependable income.

CHAPTER 2: Trading and Different between Forex, Stocks and Options

Trading refers to exchanging one object for another. When we talk about financial market trading, it's the same principle. Talk to the one who is selling stock. What they do is purchase stock or a small part of a company. If the value of those shares' increases, they gain money by selling them at a higher price again. It is merchandising. You purchase it for one price and then offer it for another again — ideally at a better price, creating a profit and vice versa. But why would the shares be worth buying? The answer is simple as the price is subject to change with the changes in supply and demand. The more there's demand for something, the more people willing to pay for it. If a business reports some impressive results and pays out nice dividends, more investors tend to purchase the company's stock. The growing competition would contribute to price rise in certain securities. Trading is about purchasing and selling for benefit in the short term. It places great emphasis on the prices.

Traders take a position in the market daily, weekly, or intraday basis intending to make short-term profits. These often concentrate on the technological aspects of a financial device rather than its long-term prospects. Traders are mainly involved in exploring the market's short-term trend and recent and rapid stock changes to leverage on it and achieve short-term profits. Timing is important in business. Traders utilize price charts to evaluate rates and price trends daily, weekly, or minute-to-minute to decipher the expected market path. Alternatively, the funds are participating in the business with a long-term perspective. They speak in terms of years and usually hold positions for over a year. Investors look for stock prospects for long-term development or profitability, but traders also take advantage of significant market demand swings that occur because of minor or large political incidents or economic news.

2.1 Trading And Different Types

Technical traders can select from five main types of trading methods. It is very important to master one trading style, but the trader also needs to be skilful in others.

Scalping

This type of day trading includes the fast and repetitive purchasing and selling within seconds or minutes of a wide quantity of stocks. Scalping is a style of trade that specializes in profiting from small changes in prices. It needs a trader to have a clear exit plan since one major failure might erase the many minor profits that the trader managed to achieve. Scalping is based on the premise that the bulk of stocks enter the first step of a trend. Yet, there is confusion on where it goes from here. Some stocks cease to progress after the initial point, while others proceed. Without making them evaporate, a scalper plans to collect as many minor gains, as necessary. It is the reverse of the mentality of "let the earnings run," which seeks to maximize successful trade results by increasing winning transactions. By raising the number of winners and reducing the value of the gains, scalping produces efficiency. A good scalper should have a significantly higher ratio of winning trades than losing ones, thus retaining gains approximately comparable to or marginally greater than losses. Traders following this technique will place ten to a few hundred orders in a single day with the hope and belief that minor changes in equity markets are simpler to spot than large ones. A short-term market position reduces the risk of running into an adverse scalping case. Scalping can be implemented as a main or supplemental trading form.

Day Trading

Day trading can be a very lucrative career if you are doing it properly. However, it can also be a little challenging for novices — especially for those who are not completely equipped for a well-planned approach. Only the most experienced day traders should be likely to encounter rough times and suffer losses. Day trading is defined as buying and selling a security within one business day. It may occur in any marketplace, but it is most common in foreign exchange (Forex) and capital markets. Day traders tend to be well-educated and well-funded. To profit on minor market swings in extremely volatile securities or currencies, they utilize large levels of leverage and short-term trading tactics. Day traders are attuned to developments that affect stock fluctuations in the short term. News-trading is a popular technique. Scheduled announcements are subject to market expectations and market psychology, such as economic statistics, corporate earnings, or interest rates. Markets react once those expectations aren't exceeded or met, usually with important, rapid movements that may benefit the day traders. Day traders use various intraday techniques. These strategies cover:

Trading in a sideways market

It focuses on buying near support and selling around resistance levels.

Trading based on news

This typically takes advantage of trading opportunities around news events due to the increased volatility.

High-frequency trading (H.F.T.)

It includes strategies using sophisticated algorithms to exploit market inefficiencies in the small or short-term.

Trading based on momentum

Momentum trading is a strategy whereby traders buy and sell depending on the severity of recent market patterns. In financial markets, momentum is determined by factors such as trading volume and corresponding price rate changes. Momentum traders assume that a rapidly rising security price in a specific direction would tend to shift in that direction before the trend loses power. Traders buy stocks with strong trends in price performance and then sell stocks whose prices do not perform well. Momentum trading can be divided into two categories:

Relative momentum strategy

This is where the turnover of various shares of a certain asset class is compared with the other. Investors will generally favor buying strong performance securities and selling weak performing securities.

Swing Trading

Swing Trading is a strategy that focuses on short-term trends in taking smaller gains and cutting losses faster. The profits can be smaller but may accumulate into outstanding annual returns when achieved continuously over time. Swing trading positions are usually held for a few days to a few weeks but may last longer. The swing trader's emphasis is not on returns that grow over weeks or months; a trade's typical period is something like 5 to 10 days. You can make many small wins in this way, which will add up to great overall returns. If you're satisfied with a gain of 20 percent for a month or more, increases of 5 or 10 percent per week or two will add up to substantial earnings.

Position Trading

Position trading is a traditional trading technique where a person keeps a long-term position in a stock, usually for months or years. Position traders disregard short-term market movements in favor of taking advantage of longer-term patterns. Position trading encompasses the longest time frame of all trading strategies. Therefore, there is a larger benefit opportunity – as well as an enhanced intrinsic risk.

2.2 Trading Markets: Forex, Stocks and Options

There are different trading markets that people trade-in based on their preferences. These are Forex Markets, Stock Markets and Options Markets. We will now explain in detail these different trading markets.

Forex

The foreign exchange market, or Forex (F.X.), is a decentralized marketplace that facilitates the purchase and sale of different currencies. This is done via the interbank market over the counter (O.T.C.) rather than on a centralized exchange. There are several reasons why traders are drawn to Forex:

- The FX-market size
- A wide range of tradable currencies
- Various volatility levels
- High rate of sale
- Trading 24 hours a day, during the week

Unlike most economies, the foreign exchange market operates such that it is responsive to demand and availability. Using a very basic example, if European citizens holding Euros demand strong for the U.S. dollar, they will exchange their Euros for Dollars. The U.S. Dollar's value will rise while the Euro's value will fall. Keep in mind that this transaction only affects the currency pair EUR / USD and, for example, will not cause the USD to depreciate against the Japanese Yen.

Triggers in the Forex Market

The example above is just one of many factors that can shift the F.X. market. These involve large macroeconomic developments such as a new president's inauguration, or country-specific indicators such as the predominant interest rate, G.D.P., unemployment, inflation, and G.D.P. debt ratio, to list just a handful. Top traders use an economic calendar to keep up with these major economic announcements that may push the sector. What's so attractive in Forex? The foreign exchange sector allows major corporations, states, retail merchants and private entities to swap one currency for another and to take effect in the interbank (between banks) system. The benefit of getting Forex trading among global banks is that Forex can be traded around the clock (throughout the week). As the Asian trading session ends, European and U.K. banks, arrive online before handing over to the U.S. The entire trade day begins as the U.S. session moves into the next day's Asian session. What makes this sector much more appealing to some traders, according to BIS Triennial Survey 2016, it is the most competitive market in the world, having an estimated regular trading amount of 5.1$ trillion. That means traders can quickly enter and exit positions because there are plenty of eager foreign exchange buyers and sellers.

Working of Forex Market

The principles behind Forex dealing are relatively straightforward. If you think a currency's value will (appreciate) go up, you'll buy the currency. This is classified as "slow-moving" You sell the currency because you fear the currency will go down (depreciate). This is regarded as "fast travel."

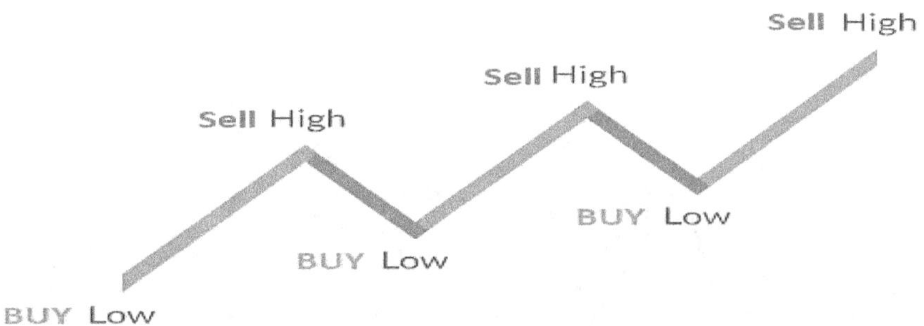

Forex Market participants

Within the foreign exchange market, there are two types of market participants. They are hedgers and speculators. Hedgers often aim to stop severe exchange-rate shifts. Think about big conglomerates like Shell and how they try to circumvent their vulnerability to fluctuations of foreign currencies. On the other hand, speculators are risk-seeking and always looking for exchange-rate volatility to profit from. They trade at the major banks and supermarkets.

Learn to Read a Forex Quote

All traders need to understand how to read a Forex quote, as this will determine the price you are entering and exiting. Looking at the currency pool below, the first currency in the EUR / USD pair is regarded as the base currency, which is the Euro, whereas the second currency in that pair (USD) is defined as the variable or quote currency.

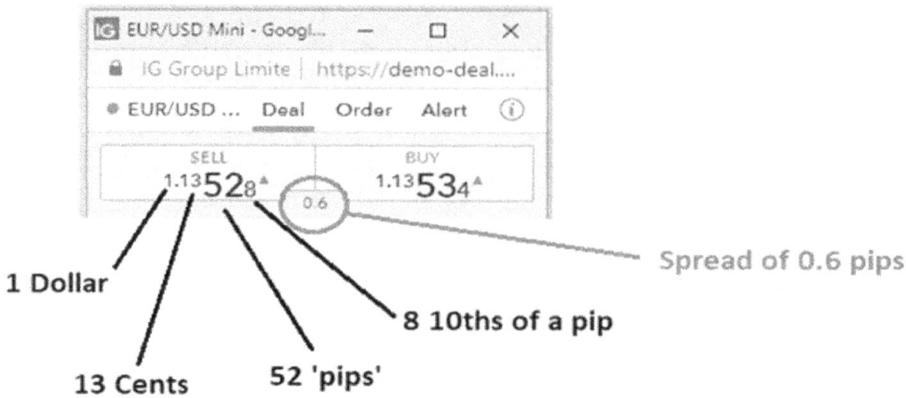

Prices are provided up to 5 decimal places for most F.X. markets, but the first four are the most significant. The number to the left of the decimal point means that the vector currency is one unit. It is the USD in this example and is, therefore, $1. The following two digits are the cents; that's 13 U.S. cents in this case. The third and fourth digits are fractions of one cent, which are called pips. It is important to note that the number is known as a 'pip' in the fourth decimal place. If the E.U.R. depreciate by 100 pips against the USD, the current sale price represents the lower price of 1.12528 because it would cost less in USD to purchase 1 Euro.

Reasons for Trading Forex

Trading Forex has many advantages over other markets, as explained below:

Low Transaction Costs

Forex traders usually make their profits out of the spread if the deal is opened and closed before any overnight funding fees are added. Forex trading stands thus cost-effective once measured counter to a market such as equities that attracts commission fees.

Low Spreads

Ask/Bid spreads are relatively small owing to the availability of big F.X. pairs. The spread is the main obstacle when dealing and needs to be resolved as the price swings in your favor. Any additional pips going in your favorite is a pure benefit.

More Profitable Opportunities

Forex trading allows traders to take speculative positions on upward (value-appreciating) and downward (value-depreciating) currencies. Additionally, many different Forex pairs are available for traders to spot profitable trades.

Leverage Trading

Forex trading involves utilizing leverage. This implies a trader will not have to pay the whole cost of the trade but can instead bring a percentage of the cost down. This can magnify your profits but also your losses. We propose a structured Risk Analysis strategy. This can be accomplished by reducing the total leverage to between 10 and one or fewer.

Forex Trading Lingo

Listed below are the key Forex trading jargons:

Base Currency

This is the first currency that appears when quoting a currency pair. Looking at EUR/USD, the Euro is the base currency.

Variable/Quote Currency

This is the second currency in the quoted currency pair and is the U.S. Dollar in the EUR/USD example.

Bid

The bid price is the highest price that a purchaser (the bidder) is prepared to pay. When you are searching to sell a Forex pair, this is the price you will notice, usually to the left of the quote. It is usually in red.

Ask

This is the opposite of the bid and indicates the lowest price a seller agrees to accept. When you are looking to buy a currency pair, this is the price you notice and is often to the right. It is usually in blue.

Spread

The disparity between the bid and the asking price is the real spread on the underlying Forex market plus the broker's added spread.

Pips/Points

A pip or point corresponds to a step in the 4th decimal position by one digit. This is also how traders respond to currency pair moves, i.e., Today, GBP / USD has raked 100 pips.

Margin

This is the amount of money that is necessary to open a leveraged position. Margin is the difference between the total value of your position and the funds that the broker lends to you.

Margin call

The margin call is triggered when the overall invested capital falls below a defined amount after adding or deducting gains or losses. Traders are then called for the replenishment of margins.

Liquidity

A currency pair is called liquid because it can be quickly acquired and exchanged since other parties participate in the currency pair.

Spot Forex

This form of Forex trading involves the purchase and sale of real money. You can buy a certain amount of pound sterling, for example, and exchange it for euros. If the pound's value is boosted, you will swap the euros for pounds again, earning more money than you used to spend on the purchase.

Long trade

If you acquire a currency, you will be conducting a long trade hoping the value will rise and profit from the disparity between the purchase price and the selling price.

Short trade

You are selling a currency intending to benefit from its current price, so you will buy it back at a lower value, gaining from the difference.

Stocks

Stocks are a form of investment in a company and a share in its profits. Investors purchase stocks to profit from their investment. Simply put, stocks are a method of accumulating wealth. You own a share of the company that issued the stock when you invest in it. Ordinary people invest in some of the world's most successful companies through stocks. Stocks are a way for businesses to raise capital.

Reason for owning stocks

When you buy a company's stock, you're effectively purchasing a partial right to the company's ownership. Is that a guarantee that you'll be seated next to Tim Cook at Apple's next shareholder meeting? No, it's not true. However, in most cases, it does imply that you have the right to vote at those meetings if you choose to do so. However, the primary motivation for stock ownership is to generate a profit. The return can result from the following two options:

- The stock's price rises. If you want, you can then sell the stock for a profit.
- Dividends are paid on the stock. Although not all stocks pay dividends, many of them do. Dividends are payments made to shareholders from a company's earnings, and they're usually made quarterly.

It is recommended to buy stock not only in one company. You must diversify your portfolio that contains stocks in many companies.

Stock Market

The word "stock market" is most used to refer to 1 of the main stock market indexes, like S& P 500 or Industrial Average of Dow Jones. Because it's difficult to keep track of every single stock, these indexes focus on a subset of the market, and their performance is regarded as representative of the entire market. You might see a news headline stating that the stock market has dropped or that the stock market has risen. Typically, this means stock market indexes have risen or fallen, implying that the stocks within the index have gained or lost value. Those who buy and sell stocks hope to profit from the fluctuation in stock prices.

Trading in Stocks

When you're ready to invest in stocks or mutual funds, you'll typically do so through the stock market, which anyone with a brokerage account can access. To invest in the stock market, you don't have to be an official "investor"; for the most part, anyone can do so. And once you've made your first investment, you'll be joining the ranks of investors all over the world who use the stock market to build long-term wealth. But first, you must understand what the stock market is, how it operates, and a few basic investment strategies.

Working of Stock Market

The stock market comprises a network of exchanges, including the New York Stock Exchange and the Nasdaq. An initial public offering, or I.P.O., is when a company sells shares of its stock on a stock exchange. Investors purchase these shares, allowing the company to raise funds to expand its operations. The exchange then tracks the supply & demand of each listed stock, allowing investors to buy and sell these stocks among themselves. The amount of every security, or the levels at which stock market participants — investors and traders — are willing to buy or sell, is influenced by supply & demand. Buyers submit a maximum amount or a "bid" they are ready to pay, which is usually less than what sellers "demand" for in trade. The bid-ask spread is the name for this difference. A buyer must raise his price, or a seller must lower hers for a trade. When buying stock, you'll see the bid, ask, and bid-ask spread on your broker's website, but the difference in most cases will be pennies so that it won't be a big deal for beginners and long-term investors.

Know-How to Invest in Stock Market

Individual stocks can be purchased using a brokerage account or an individual retirement account (I.R.A.). You can open both accounts with an online broker and use them to buy and sell investments. The broker serves as an intermediary between you and the stock exchanges. Online brokerages have simplified the signup process, and once you've funded your account, you can choose the right investments for you. There are risks associated with any investment. On the other hand, stocks carry higher risk — and a higher potential reward — than other investments.

Options

A derivative is a contract that gives the buyer the right, but not the obligation, to buy or sell the underlying asset at a specified price by a certain date (expiration date) (strike price). Calls and puts are the two types of options. Options in the American style can be exercised at any time before they expire. Only on the expiration date can European-style options be exercised. Options and options trading is explained in detail in the ensuing chapter.

2.3 Difference Between Forex, Stocks and Options

Explained below are the key differences between the different markets based on their features:

24 Hours trading

Compared to Options and Stocks trading, one advantage of the Forex Exchange Trading Systems (Forex) is the capability to trade twenty-four hours a day, five days a week if desired. The Forex market is open for the longest period of any market. It's great to have unlimited time each week to make trades if your goal is to make double-digit gains in a market. When a major event occurs worldwide, you can be among the first to profit from the situation by using Forex Trading. You won't have to wait for a market to open in the morning, as you would with Options or Stocks. You can trade at any time of day or night from the comfort of your computer.

Trade Execution

You get immediate trade executions when you use the Forex Currency Trading System. There is no lag, as there can be in Options, Stocks, or other markets. And instead of guessing which price your order will be filled at, your order will be filled at the best possible price. Your order will not "slip" as it might with Options. There is a lot more liquidity in Forex Trading than in Options Trading to help with "slippage."

Liquidity

Like Stocks and Options Trading, Forex Trading has the advantage of being more liquid than any other market. There is no comparison with the Forex Market, which has an average daily volume of close to 2 trillion dollars. Foreign currency trading (Forex) has far more liquidity than the stock and options markets. This means that Forex traders will be much easier to fill than Options trades when trading. This increased speed equates to a higher potential profit. When you combine this with

Forex Trading's instantaneous trade execution, you can quickly make many trades.

Commissions

Because Forex or F.X. trading is an interbank market that matches buyers and sellers in real-time, there are no commissions. Unlike other markets, there are no middleman brokerage fees. There is a spread among the ask prices & bid, wherever Forex trading organizations make a little of their money. This means that when you trade Forex, you may save money compared to stock and options trading, where commissions are charged because you are dealing with a brokerage firm.

Greater Leverage

Compared to stock and options trading, online forex trading can provide you with a lot more leverage. On the other hand, options allow you to manage putt and call options so that you greatly increase your leverage. When you know what a currency is going to do, leverage can be very useful. When it comes to Forex, you can make a lot more money if you make the right move.

Limited Risk

Because Forex traders should set limits on their positions, the probability is limited because the online competencies of Forex Trading systems inevitably initiate the margin call when the margin amount exceeds the account value in dollars. This prevents any Forex trader from losing a huge amount of money if the market turns against them. It's an excellent safety feature that isn't always present in some other financial markets. In addition, Forex differs from Options in that you only have a limited amount of time to trade before the options expire.

CHAPTER 3: What is Options trading?

The Chicago Board Options Exchange has defined options as:

The option is some contract that gives the buyer the right, but never the obligation, to buy or sell an underlying asset (such as an index or stock) at a certain price on & before the specific date. Like a bond, an option is an option

That definition could just be written in ancient Greek for most casual investors. On the other hand, brokers occasionally buy and sell options for investors who have no idea what they are, can't appreciate or afford the risk, and may not even be aware that the transactions are taking place. Contracts that give the owner the right to sell or buy an asset at a set price for a set period are known as options. Depending on the type of options contract, the said period could be as brief as a day or as lengthy as a couple of years. Trading options are easy to grasp once you've mastered a few key concepts. Multiple asset classes are commonly used in investor portfolios. Stocks, bonds, ETFs, and even mutual funds are examples of these. When used correctly, options are another asset class that provides many benefits that trading stocks and ETFs alone cannot. Options are traded on a variety of underlying assets. Options can be used in various ways, including to speculate or mitigate risk, and they can be traded on a variety of underlying securities. Equities, indexes, and exchange-traded funds (ETFs) are the most popular underlying securities (Exchange Traded Funds). There are several distinctions between index-based options and those based on equities as well as ETFs. Before you begin trading, it's critical to understand the differences. Trading options is all about taking calculated risks. If statistics and probability are your greatest strengths, volatility and trading options are likely to be as well.

3.1 What Is Options Trading?

Options trading is simply the act of trading options on securities traded on the stock or bond markets (along with ETFs and the like). To begin, you must use a brokerage to buy or sell options. The strike price of a call option for a stock, for instance, will be decided based on the stock's current price when purchased. For example, if a stock's share price is $1,540, any strike price (the price of a call option) that is higher than that stock's share price is considered "out of the money." In contrast, if the strike price is less than the current stock price, it is said to be "in the money." The opposite is true for put options (right to sell): strike prices that are below the current share price are considered "out of the money," and vice versa.

What's more, any "out of the money" options- whether call or put- will be worthless when they expire (this means that you need to have an "in the money" option while trading on the stock market). Call options are usually bullish, whereas put options are normally bearish. Fridays are when most options expire, but there are some exceptions (for instance, monthly, bi-monthly, quarterly, etc.). Six-month contracts are common in option contracts.

3.2 Historical and Implied Volatility

You only need to worry about two types of volatility as an individual trader: historical volatility and implied volatility. In options trading, volatility refers to the magnitude of a stock's price swings. As you might expect, high volatility in securities (such as stocks) equates to higher risk, while low volatility equates to lower risk. Stocks with high volatility (those whose share prices fluctuate a lot) are more expensive when trading options on the stock market than those with low volatility. However, owing to the erratic nature of the stock market, even low volatility stocks could become high volatility ones ultimately).

3.2.1 Options and Historical Volatility

Historical volatility depicts how much the stock price fluctuates daily over one year in the past. Because it quantifies how much a stock fluctuates daily over one-year, historical volatility is an excellent measure of volatility. On the other hand, implied volatility assesses a stock's (or security's) future volatility depending on the market during the option contract's life.

3.2.2 Options and Implied Volatility

Implied volatility is incumbent on what the market is implying the stock's volatility would be in the future, over the option contract's life. One of the most key concepts for options traders to grasp is implied volatility, which can help you decide the probability of a stock reaching a particular price by a certain date. It can also be used to predict how volatile the market will be in the future.

3.5 Types of Options

There are only two types of options available: "put" and "call." These are commonly referred to as "puts" and "calls." You can buy or sell as many option contracts as you want, but each contract handles 100 shares of stock. It's important to note that the owner of either a call or a put option contract is under no obligation to exercise her or his right to buy or sell.

3.5.1 Call Options

A call option contract gives the holder the right to buy 100 shares of a specific security at a specific price and within a certain time frame. When you buy a call option, you're buying the right to buy 100 shares of a specific stock from the option's seller at a predetermined price, known as the "strike price." If you don't use the call by a particular date, it will expire. To buy a call option, you must pay a fee to the call's seller, known as a "premium." When you buy a call option, you're hoping that the stock's market price that you're buying will rise shortly. What is the reason for this? If the stock price rises above the strike price, you could indeed exercise the call and buy the stock from the call's seller at the strike price or a price lower than the stock market value. Then you have the option of keeping the shares (which you got for a good price) or selling them for a profit. But what occurs if the stock price falls instead of rising? Your loss is restricted to the cost of the premium because you let the call option expire.

3.5.2 Put Options

A put option contract gives the holder the right to sell 100 shares of a specific security at a certain price within a certain time frame. When you purchase a put option, you are purchasing the right to compel the person who sells you the put to buy 100 shares of a specific stock from you at the strike price. You want the stock price to fall below the strike price when you hold put options. If it does, the put seller will be obligated to purchase shares from you at the strike price. The said strike price would be higher than the current market price. A put option resembles the insurance policy in contradiction of the shares losing much value because you can force the option seller to purchase your shares at a price above market value. If the market price rises rather than falls, your shares will appreciate, and you can easily let the option expire, as you will only lose the premium you paid for the put.

3.6 Selling and Buying a Put Option

You can produce double-digit income & returns by selling put options even in an overvalued, flat, or bearish market. For big returns on investment, you do not require quick business growth or any solid bull market. In the case of a market collapse, you may even grant your investments a 10 percent guarantee against the downside. In other words, if the market falls by 25%, your equity positions are likely to fall by only 15%. You can also enter stock positions exactly at the price you want and keep the cost base low. You should try to purchase in a declining market to get a greater bargain instead of buying at presently available market rates. There is a perfect period and place for selling put options like any device, and at certain times it is not an optimal strategy. This is a sophisticated and best way of entering equity positions when used correctly.

To option sellers, the two most critical things are the strike and the bid. The strike is the amount you agree to buy the shares for if the option is exercised, and the bid is about the amount you can expect to earn on selling the option. If you sell an option with a strike price of $30 below the current stock price of $30.50, you will now receive $143 from the option buyer, and you will be obliged to purchase 100 shares of the company at $30 each if the buyer wishes, for a total of $3,000, at any time before the option expires in 3.5 months.

Suppose the company's stock generally stays above $30 / share over the next 3.5 months. In that case, the option buyer probably won't assign the shares to you, as there would be no reason for her to force you to pay exactly $30 / share when the market price is already above $30 / share. Her option will expire worthlessly, you will keep your $143 premium, and your $3,000 in secured cash will be released for another option to be sold. Here is the calculated rate of return, if the right expires: $143 / $2,857 = 0.05 = 5%

After around 3.5 months, you made a return yield of 5 percent on your initial currency. This will be around 18 percent annualized returns on your investment if you practice that for the remainder of the year a few times. Compare this with the historical return of the S&P 500 of around 9%. Compared to average stock returns, you're being charged a huge amount of money to only hang around and wait for a market drop on a business you'd like to buy. On the contrary, if the stock dips to $29.50 / share, you still must retain the $143 premium, and the buyer option will assign you to purchase the 100 shares for $30 each.

This means that your effective cost base for buying those shares was only $28.57, which, as you wanted, is below your target buy price. You ended up having to purchase them for $30 apiece, but you still got a $1.43 / share bonus upfront, which covered some of the expense. The total cost structure is that for 100 securities, you must spend $28.57 / share, or $2.857. So instead, you hold 100 shares of a company already selling for $29.50 each. You purchased a wonderful business at a decent price, and ideally, you should still anticipate lots of growth in profits and dividends over time.

3.7 Basics of Option Contracts

Let us understand the salient of call and options contracts and trading mechanisms.

3.8 Salient of Call Option

The following components contain the major characteristics of an option:

Strike Price

When a derivative contract is exercised, the strike price is the price to be bought or sold. The strike price for call options is the price at which the option holder can purchase the security; the strike price for put options is the price at which the security could be sold. The exercise price is another name for the strike price. The strike price of put and call options is an important factor to consider. A stock option call, for example, gives the buyer the right but not the obligation to purchase the stock at the strike price in the future.

Similarly, a stock option put buyer has the right but not the obligation to sell the stock at the strike price in the future. The most significant aspect of the option value is the strike or exercise price. When a contract is first written, strike prices are established. It informs the investor of the price at which the fundamental asset should trade for the option to be into money (ITM). Strike values are standardized, which means they are set at specific dollar amounts, such as $41, $42, $43, $102, $105, and so on. The value of an option is determined by the price gap between the underlying stock price and the strike price. If the strike price of a call option is higher than the underlying stock price, the option is out of the money for the buyer (OTM). The option may still have value based on volatility and time until expiration in this case. This is because that these two factors can put the option in the money in the future. If an underlying stock value is higher than the strike price, an option would possess intrinsic value & will also be profitable. When the underlying stock price is under the strike price, the purchaser of the put option is in the money, and when the underlying stock price is over the strike price, the buyer is out of the money. An OTM option will not possess intrinsic value; however, it might have value depending on the underlying asset's volatility and the remaining time until expiration.

Premium

The cost of the option, for either the buyer or the seller

Expiration

When the option runs out and is settled

3.9 Salient of Put Option

A put option contract gives the owner the right to sell security within a given time frame within a given time frame . Each contract represents 100 share or the stock on which the option is based. Putting options enables traders to magnify downward market changes, transforming a slight price decline into a big benefit for the put buyer.

Trading Calls and Puts

Buying stock provides a long position for you. Buying a call option will give you a potentially long position in the underlying stock. Short selling stock provides you with a short position. Selling a naked or uncovered call in the underlying stock gives you a potential short position. Buying a put option in the underlying stock gives you a potentially short position. Selling a put option gives you a theoretically long place in the stock underlying it. Those who purchase options are classified as investors, and others who offer options are named options writers. Here's the big difference between holders and writers. There is no requirement to call investors and put investors (buyers) to buy or sell. They are granted the opportunity to exercise their privileges. This reduces the chance of options owners just paying the premium. However, call writers and put writers (sellers) are obliged to buy or sell if the option expires. This means a seller may need to make good on a purchase or sell pledge. It also means that sellers of options are subject to additional, infinite threats in certain situations. It ensures writers will risk a lot more than the quality of premium options.

Buying a call option is betting that the price of a share of security (such as a stock or index) will rise over a set period. If you purchase a call option for Alphabet (AOOG) at $1,500 and are bullish on the stock, you forecast that the stock's price will rise. When you buy put options, you're betting that the underlying security's price will fall over time (so you're pessimistic about the stock). For example, if you buy a put option on the S&P 500 at $1,800 per share, you are bearish on the stock market and believe the S&P 500 will fall in value over time (perhaps to $1,500). Because you bought the put option when the index was at $1,800 per share (supposing the strike price was at or near that level), you'd be able to sell it for the same price (not the new, lower price). The price of the underlying security, the time until the option expires, and the volatility of the underlying security all influence option trading (especially in the stock market). The option's premium (price) is determined by the option's intrinsic value and its time value (extrinsic value).

3.10 Time Value and In the Money, At the Money and Out of the Money

In the Money

Let us understand the concepts related to options' time value, in the money, at the money and out of the money.

In the Money

If you buy an option that is already "in the money" (indicating it will profit right away), the premium will be higher because you will be able to sell it right away for a profit. In the case of call options, contracts that are "in the money" are those with an underlying asset price (ETF, stock, etc.) then strike price. If the put option's strike price is less than the current price of the underlying asset, the contract will be "in the money" (stock, ETF, etc.)

At the Money

If you have an option that is "at the money," on the other hand, the option is equal to the current stock price. And, as you might expect, an option that is "out of the money" will have no added value since it is currently not profitable.

Out of the Money

You can sell options to collect a time premium if an option (whether a put or call option) proceeds to be "out of the money" around its expiration date.

Time Value in Options

The time value, also known as the extrinsic value, is the value of an option greater than its intrinsic value-or, above the "in the money" area. The more time an option has before it expires, the more time it must make a profit, so its premium (price) will be higher due to its higher time value. In contrast, the less time an options contract has until it expires, the lower its time value. This is because the less additional time value would be added to the premium). In other words, the more time an option has before expiration, the more time value would be added to the premium (price), and the less time it has before actual expiration, the less time value would be added to the premium (price).

3.11 In options trading, the Option traders borrow from the Greeks

Options traders use the Greek Alphabet to refer to how option prices are anticipated to change in the market. This is crucial to trading success. Gamma, Delta, and Theta are the most referenced. The values are theoretical, but they would help describe the key factors driving movement in option pricing and collectively suggest how the marketplace expects an option's price to change. There never is a 100% assurance that these predictions will be accurate to put it another way.

3.12 Option trading starts with your financial goals

Like many experienced traders, Options traders have a good understanding of the financial goals and optimal market position. The way you approach and think about money, in general, will influence how you trade options. Before you finance your account and begin trading, the greatest thing you could do is define your investment objectives.

3.13 Option traders speak their lingo

You can sell a put or buy a call when trading options. You can be tall or short, and your height has nothing to do with it. As a result, you can be in-the-money, at-the-money, or out-of-the-money. In a room full of option traders, those are just a few of the popular words you'll hear.

3.14 Pros and Cons

One of the most appealing aspects of options trading is its purported safety. Options are often more resilient to market price changes (and downturns), could really help increase income on present and future investments, will often get you better deals on a variety of equities, and, maybe most importantly, could even help you capitalize on that equity rising or falling over time without having to invest in it directly, according to Nasdaq's options trading tips. Trading options, of course, have drawbacks, one of which is a risk. Risks involved with options trading can be interpreted in various ways, but they mainly revolve around the market's volatility or uncertainty. Expensive options, for example, have a high level of uncertainty, implying that the market for that asset is volatile and trading it is risky.

3.15 Striking Characteristics of Options

Options, like other types of assets, can be purchased through a brokerage account. Options are powerful because they can help an individual's portfolio. They do so by providing additional income, protection, and even leverage. Depending on the situation, there is usually a scenario of options tailored to an investor's target. A popular example of limiting downside losses is to use options as a beneficial hedge against a falling stock market. Options could also be used to produce recurring income.

Furthermore, they are frequently used for gambling purposes, such as betting on stock direction. Options trading entails certain risks, which the investor should be aware of before making a trade. Options come with risks and are therefore not suitable for everyone. Option trading is inherently risky and carries a high risk of failure.

- The option is some contract that gives the purchaser the right but not the obligation- to sell or buy an underlying resource at a specified price on or before a certain date.
- Options are also known as derivatives because they derive value from the underlying assets. • Traders use income, speculation, and risk-hedging options.
- While a stock option contract usually contains 100 percent of the underlying stock, options can be written on various underlying properties, including debt, currency, and product.

Options Provide a Hedge Against Losses

Purchasing options can provide a hedge against losses, and they can be used prudently in this regard. However, numerous options strategies are little more than gambling and therefore can significantly increase your risk. The sale of "uncovered" calls is a simple example. Remember that when exercising a call, the seller of the call must deliver stock. If you sell a call on a stock, you already have, the call is "covered" by those shares, and you've already paid for it. You'll simply deliver the shares to the option holder if the option is exercised. However, if you sell an "uncovered" call, which means you don't yet own the stock, your loss potential is limitless. If you exercise your option, you'll have to purchase the shares on the open market to meet your obligation, regardless of how high the price is at the time. If the share price has risen sharply due to a strong market upside movement or a significant announcement by the issuer, your losses could be massive.

3.16 Drawbacks of Options Trading

Given below are some of the disadvantages of options trading that must be considered, especially by beginners.

Options Expose Sellers to Extreme Losses

Contrary to an option buyer (or holder)-losses of much greater value- than the contract's price- can be incurred by the option seller (writer). Remember, when an investor opts to write a put or call at a predetermined price, he or she is required to purchase or sell shares within the time frame irrespective of whether the price is in his favor or against.

Options Are Time-Specific

Short term is the basic essence of options. Investors of options seek to benefit from a near-term market change that could take place for the trade/contract to generate payoff within days, weeks, or months. This requires two correct decisions: determining the best time to obtain the option contract and determining specifically whether to exercise, sell or step away before the offer expires. There isn't a deadline for long-term equity buyers. They have time to let their investment play out for years, even decades.

Pre-Requisites for Potential Traders

You must apply for clearance from your broker before even starting trading options. The broker may grant you a trading class that determines what kinds of options trades you are permitted to place after addressing several questions regarding your financial capital, investing background and your knowledge on the inherent risks of trading options. Any trader who is into options trading must hold in their trading account a minimum of $2,000, which is an industry-standard and a cost of investment worth contemplating.

Options' Trading Involves Additional Costs

Any trading strategy for options (such as selling call options on stocks you don't own) enables buyers to set up a margin account, which is simply a line of credit that acts as collateral if the transaction shifts against the investor. For the opening of a margin account, each brokerage company has various minimum conditions and may base the sum and interest rate on how much cash and shares are in the account. Usually, margin loan interest rates may range between the low single digits and the low double digits. If an investor is unwilling to make good on loan (or if the value of the trading account falls below a certain amount, which may happen due to regular market fluctuations), if he or she does not add more cash or securities to it, the lender may trigger a margin call and liquidate an investor's portfolio. The Options Clearing Corporation offers a comprehensive overview of the features and risks of standardized options and an overview of the U.S. federal income tax rules that impact those looking to invest in options and other financial products.

Bottom line

You must recognize the company's market inside out and determine whether to purchase, sell or retain stock for the long term and have a good understanding of the way the asset is going. Investors of options ought to be hyper-aware of those items and more. Success in options demands from investors to have a clear idea of the inherent value of the firm, but perhaps most significantly, they will need to have a sound thesis of how the business has been and would be impacted by short-term variables such as internal activities, sector/competition, and macroeconomic impacts. Many investors may conclude that options expose their financial lives to an excessive amount of risk. However, if you are interested in exploring the possibilities that options offer and have the discipline and capital to withstand potential losses, the options trading strategies for beginners can help limit your downside. Many options strategies are extremely complicated and risky. As a result, not all options strategies are appropriate for all investors. Writing puts or uncovered calls would be unsuitable for almost everyone, except for sophisticated, high-net-worth individuals who can afford and are willing to incur significant losses. Nonetheless, brokers occasionally engage in inappropriate options trading on behalf of customers who do not understand the risks. The next chapter is dedicated to various strategies that can be applied successfully for making money in trading options.

CHAPTER 4: Trading Strategy for New Options Traders

When you trade options, the contracts usually take the following form:

The stock ticker (the name of the stock), the expiration date (typically in mm/dd/yy, though dates are sometimes flipped with the year first, month second, and day in the end), the call or put, strike price and the premium price (for instance, $4) are all listed on the contract. As an illustration of a call option for Apple stock, consider the following: APPL 01/15/2018 200 Call @ 4.

Regardless, the option trade would then look very different depending on which platform you are trading on. When trading options, you have various strategies to choose from, all of which differ in terms of risk, reward, and other factors. While there are dozens of strategies (the majority of which are complex), here are a few key ones that have been advised for beginners.

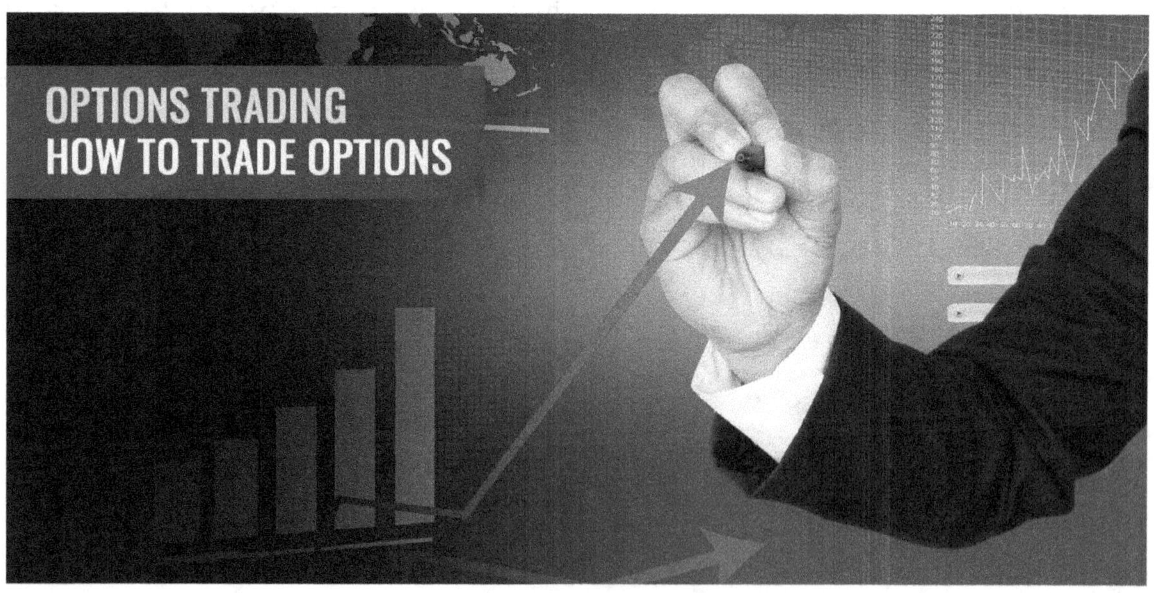

4.1 Straddles

When trading straddles (long in this case), you expect the asset (like stock) to be extremely volatile, but you don't know which way it will go (up or down). You buy a call and a put option at the same strike price, underlying price, and expiry date when using a straddle strategy. This strategy is commonly used when a trader expects a company's stock to decline or skyrocket in response to an event such as an earnings report. When a company like Apple (AAPL) is preparing to release 3rd-quarter earnings on August 31st, an options trader can use a straddle strategy to buy a call option that expires on the date at the current Apple stock price, as well as a put option that expires on the same day at the same price.

4.2 Strangles

An investor will buy an "out of the money" call and an "out of the money" put for almost the same expiry date for almost the same underlying asset in a strangle (long in this example). Investors using this strategy believe the underlying asset (such as stock) will experience a significant price change, but they don't know how it will go. A long strangle is a relatively safe trade because the investor only requires the stock to move more than the total premium paid, regardless of which direction it moves. The advantage of a strangle strategy there is much less risk of loss because the premiums are lower because the options are "out of the money," which means they are less expensive to purchase.

4.3 Covered Call

A covered call is a good choice for you if you have long asset investments (such as stocks). This strategy is best for investors who are only slightly bullish or neutral on a stock. A covered call is created by purchasing 100 shares of regular stock and selling one call option/100 shares. This type of strategy can help you lower the risk of the current stock investments while also allowing you to profit from the option. When the stock price rises or remains relatively constant over the life of the option contract, covered calls could make you money. However, if the stock price falls too far, you could lose money on this trade. However, there is a probability of making money, provided it does take a little dip. However, by employing this strategy, you can protect your investment from share price declines while also allowing yourself to profit while the stock price remains stable.

4.4 Selling Iron Condors

The trader's risk can be conservative or risky based on their preference for this strategy. The trade's position for iron condors is non-directional, meaning the asset-like a stock- could go up or down, with profit potential over a wide range. To use this strategy, sell a put as well as buy another put at a lower strike price (basically a put spread), then combine it with buying a call as well as selling a call at a higher strike price (essentially a call spread) (a call spread). The puts and calls are short. You profit when the stock price remains between the two puts or calls (so even if the price fluctuates slightly, you profit). However, the strategy results in a loss when the stock price rises or falls dramatically above or below the spreads. As a result, the iron condor is thought to be in a market-neutral position.

4.5 Collars

A collar option technique, also known as a hedge wrapper or just collar, is an options strategy used to minimize an underlying asset's positive and negative returns. It restricts the portfolio's return to a defined range and may hedge the position against the underlying asset's potential volatility. The use of a protective put, and covered call option produces a collar position. It is produced more precisely by keeping an underlying stock, purchasing an option that is out of the money, and selling an option out of the money call.

How to create a Collar Position

The collar position is created by using the following method:

Collar Position=Long Underlying Asset + Long Put Option + Short Call Option

4.6 Combinations

A combination is an options trading strategy that entails purchasing and selling calls and putting options on the same underlying stock.

4.7 Call buying strategy

When you buy a call option, you get the right to buy the underlying futures contract at the strike price at any time before the contract expires. This happens infrequently, and there is little benefit in doing so. Most traders purchase call options since they assume a commodity market will rise, so they want to profit from it. You can also close the option before it expires, but only during market hours. You must first determine your goals before deciding on the best purchase option. When purchasing call options, keep the following in mind:

You must determine the time you plan to remain in the call option trade

Many commodities and futures offer various options in terms of expiration months and strike prices, allowing you to choose an option that meets your needs. This will assist you in determining the amount of time required for a call option. You should buy a commodity with a minimum of two weeks remaining on it if you expect a commodity to finish its move higher within two weeks. If you only plan on being in the trade for a few weeks, you should avoid buying an option with six to nine months remaining because the options will be more expensive as well as you will lose some leverage. One thing to keep in mind is that option time premiums decay more quickly in the last 30 days. As a result, you could be correct in your trade assumptions, but the option loses much more time value, and you lose money. We recommend buying an option for 30 more days than you anticipate being in the trade.

Plan the Amount You Want to Invest in Buying A Call Option

Some options could be too expensive for you to purchase, or they may not be the right options at all, depending on the size of your account and your risk tolerances. Options would be more expensive in the money call than out of the money call. Also, the longer the call options are available, they'll cost. When you buy most options, in contrast to futures contracts, there is a margin. The entire option premium must be paid upfront. As a result, options in volatile markets such as crude oil can cost thousands of dollars. That may not be appropriate for all options traders, and you don't want to repeat the error of buying options that are far out of the money just because they are within your price range. The majority of deep out of the money options could well expire worthless, making them long shots.

Length of A Move You Expect from The Market

You must have an idea about the type of move you anticipate from the commodity or futures market to optimize your leverage and control your risk. Buying in the money options is usually the more conservative approach. Buying multiple contracts of out-of-the-money options is a more aggressive strategy. If the market makes a large move higher, out-of-the-money multiple options contracts will increase your returns. It's also riskier because you're more likely to lose your entire option premium if the market doesn't move.

Work out the breakeven point on buying call options

It is worked out as follows:

Strike Price + Option Premium Paid

This formula is used at option expiration because there is no time value left on the call options. If the options are deep in the money or far out of the money, you can sell the options at any time before expiration and keep the time premium.

Determine your stop-loss

For a short position, a call option can also be used as a low-risk stop-loss instrument. Stops for risk positions are recommended for traders and investors in volatile markets. A stop is a risk-reward function; you must never risk more on any investment than you intend to make.

Stops have the drawback of causing the market to trade to a level that triggers a stop but then reverse. A long call option serves as stop-loss protection for those with short positions, but it can give you more time than a stop that closes the position when it reaches the risk level because the call option serves two purposes if the option has time left when the market becomes volatile.

- The call option would also act as price insurance for the short position, shielding it from further losses above the strike price.
- More importantly, the call option helps you to keep your position short even if the price rises above the insured level or strike price.

Markets frequently rise only to reverse course and plummet after stop orders are triggered. The call option will then keep a market participant in a short position if the option has time until expiration, allowing them to survive a volatile period before the market returns to a downtrend. A short position combined with a long call is primarily the same as a low risk long put position. Call options are instruments that can be used to take a direct position in a market to bet on the price rising or to safeguard an existing short position from a price rise.

4.8 Getting started with trading options

We have explained below in simple steps the process of starting trading options.

Open an options trading account

- You must first open an options trading account before you can begin trading options. Opening an options trading account necessitates a larger sum of money. Brokerage firms evaluate potential options traders based on their trading experience, risk awareness, and financial preparedness. The details will be recorded in an options trading agreement submitted to your prospective broker for approval. You'll need to provide the following details:

- Investment objectives
- Trading experience
- Personal financial information
- The types of options you want to trade

The broker will usually assign you an initial trading level based on your answers and the level of risk you are willing to take-typically 1 to 5, where 1 is the lowest risk, and 5 is the highest). This is how you'll be able to make certain types of options trades.

Pick which options to buy or sell

What type of options contract to take depends on which direction you anticipate the underlying stock to move?

- Buy a call option and sell a put option if you believe the stock price will rise.
- Sell a call option or a put option if you believe the stock price will remain stable.
- Buy a put option and sell a call option if you believe the stock price will fall.

Predict the option strike price

Purchasing an option is recommended if the stock price closes the options' expiration period "in the money. That is, the price must be below or above the strike price. You should purchase an option with a strike price that matches where you believe the stock will be during the option's lifetime. The premium, or the price you pay for an option, comprises two parts- time value and intrinsic value. If the stock price is above the strike, intrinsic value is the gap between the strike price and the share price. What's left is called time value, and it considers things like the stock's volatility, the time until expiration, as well as interest rates, in addition to other things.

Determine the option time frame

Every options contract has an expiration date that indicates when you could exercise the option. There are 2 types of options: American and European, which differ in terms of when they can be implemented. The American option might be applied at any time until expiration date, but European options could just be implemented on the day of expiration. Because American options give the option buyer more flexibility (and the option seller more risk), they are usually more expensive than the European counterparts. Expiration dates can be anything from a few days to a few months to a few years. Daily as well as weekly options are the riskiest and should only be used by experienced option traders. Monthly as well as yearly expiration dates are preferable for long-term investors. Longer expiration dates give the stock more time to move, as well as more time for the investment thesis to come to fruition. The longer the expiration period, the more expensive the option will be.

4.9 Trading Rules

Listed below are the trading rules both for the professional traders and the beginners:

- Divide the capital into some equal parts (if possible 10) & never risk higher than 1 share of the capital on a single trade.

- Trade just in stocks, options and currencies which are active and liquid
- Use the stop-losses
- Never over-trade and stick to guidelines regarding risk management
- Never let gains become losses
- Use trail stops to secure your money, and lock them
- Never trade in a rush
- Never get out of the market just because you've lost faith
- Don't guess where the tops and bottoms of the market are, but let the top and bottom of the market indicate
- Never average the losing trade
- Stop taking large losses and low gains
- Pay attention to risk factor
- Always trade within your capacities, financially and otherwise
- Never allow greed or fear to take hold of your winning positions

Avoid tips & rumors because people with vested interests spread these tips

4.10 Common Options Trading Mistakes

There are plenty of mistakes that can be committed even by the professional while trading options. These are:

- Selling for thrill & excitement
- High ego involved in trading.
- Risking money, you cannot afford to lose
- Too passionate about money
- Absence of trade system and lack of record-keeping
- Not allowing profits to run

- Allowing losses to increase
- Letting minor losses become major losses
- Not sticking to plans & strategies
- Anti-trend trading – short-selling on the bull market and going long on the bear market

4.11 Technical analysis for trading Options

In short-term trading, technical indicators enable the investor to recognize the trend and its trajectory. Since options are prone to time decay, the retention period takes on value. A stock trader can retain a position forever, while an options trader is constrained by the fixed time specified by the expiry date of the options. Due to time constraints, momentum indicators are common among options traders, which appear to identify overbought and oversold levels.

Relative Strength Index – R.S.I.

For options on specific securities, R.S.I. fits well. The strongest candidates for short-term trading dependent on R.S.I. are the options for extremely liquid, high-beta stocks.

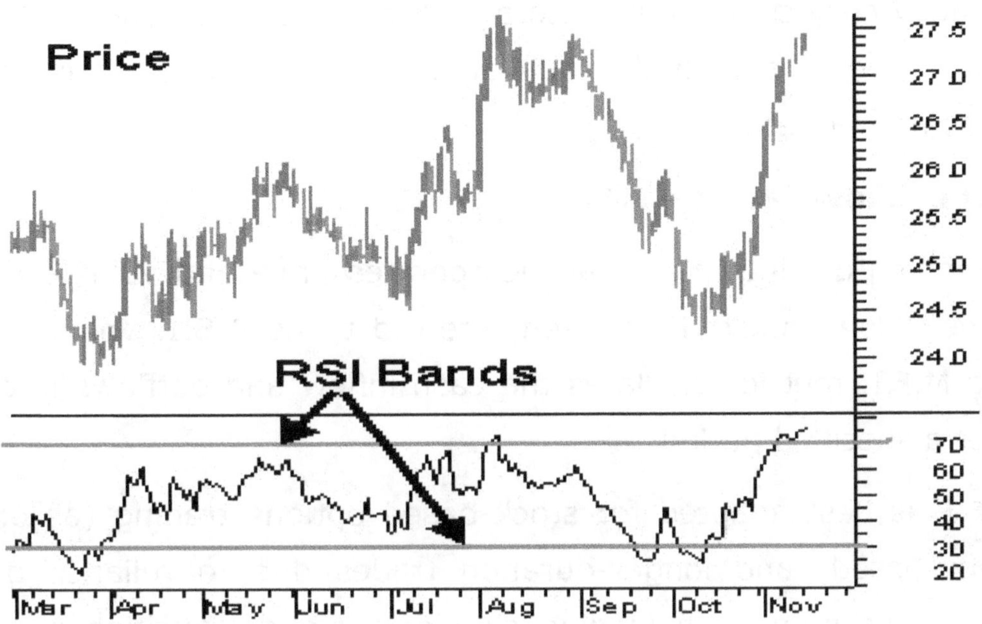

Bollinger Bands

The worth of volatility seems to be known to each options trader, & Bollinger band is amongst the most common approaches for calculating volatility. When volatility rises, the bands extend and contract when volatility declines. The more the price travels to the upper band, the more the security can be overbought, and the more the price rises to the lower band, the more it may be oversold. A shift of prices beyond the bands will indicate that the security is ripe for a turnaround, and traders of options should position themselves appropriately.

Intraday Momentum Index – I.M.I.

For high-frequency option traders seeking to gamble on intraday movements, an Intraday Momentum Index is a strong technical indicator. This incorporates the intraday candlesticks & R.S.I. principles, thereby providing the acceptable range to intraday trading (like R.S.I.) by suggesting degrees of overbought and oversold. Utilizing I.M.I., an options trader could be able to spot possible opportunities at an intraday correction to execute a bullish trade in an up-trending market or to execute a bearish trade at an intraday price bump in a down-trending market.

Money Flow Index – MFI

A momentum indicator that incorporates price and volume data is the Money Flow Index. It is often referred to as R.S.I. volume weighted. The M.F.I. metric calculates the cash inflow and outflows into an asset over a specified period.

M.F.I. is best adapted for stock-based options trading (as opposed to index-based) and longer-duration trades due to reliance on volume data. This may be a leading sign of a trend transition as the M.F.I. moves in the same direction as the stock price.

Put-Call Ratio (PCR) Indicator

Using put options against call options, the put-call ratio calculates trading volume. Regardless of the actual put-call ratio's value, the shifts in its value signify a shift in general market sentiment.

The ratio is above 1 when there are more puts than calls, suggesting bearishness. The ratio is less than 1, suggesting bullishness, while call volume is greater than put volume. The put-call ratio, however, is often regarded by traders as a contrary measure.

Open Interest – O.I.

Open interest shows possibilities for open or unsettled contracts. O.I. does not generally imply a particular uptrend or downtrend, but it does include indicators of a given trend's intensity. Rising open interest implies fresh capital inflow and the current trend's longevity, while a slowing pattern implies a declining O.I.

Conclusion

Because options are a type of derivative, their value is determined by the underlying instrument's price. A stock can be the underlying instrument. However, other underlying instruments like an index, a currency, a commodity, or any other security could be. An option contract is a financial contract that gives an investor the option to sell or buy a specific asset at a predetermined price by a certain date. It does, however, include the right to purchase but not the obligation to do so. When it comes to an understanding the meaning of an option contract, it's important to remember that there are 2 parties involved: a buyer (also known as the holder) and a seller (also known as the writer). There are 2 types of options available. These are referred to as the call and put options. Contract size, premium or down payment, Strike price, Expiration date, Intrinsic value, Settlement of an option, and no obligation to buy or sell are all features of an option contract. Then, American options could be implemented until the expiration date, while European options might only be implemented. At the NSE, all index options appear as European options. Anyone interested in trading options should have a basic understanding of how options are priced. Several factors determine the options' value. The intrinsic value, current stock price, the time to expiration, the time value, and other factors such as volatility, interest rates, and so on are among them. Options have several advantages. These have a low cost of entry because, unlike stock transactions, they allow an investor and trader to take a position with a small sum of money. Another benefit of options is that they provide risk hedging. Options trading is also more flexible as compared to any other type of trading. Options work in all kinds of market conditions and are a valuable and profitable trading instrument.